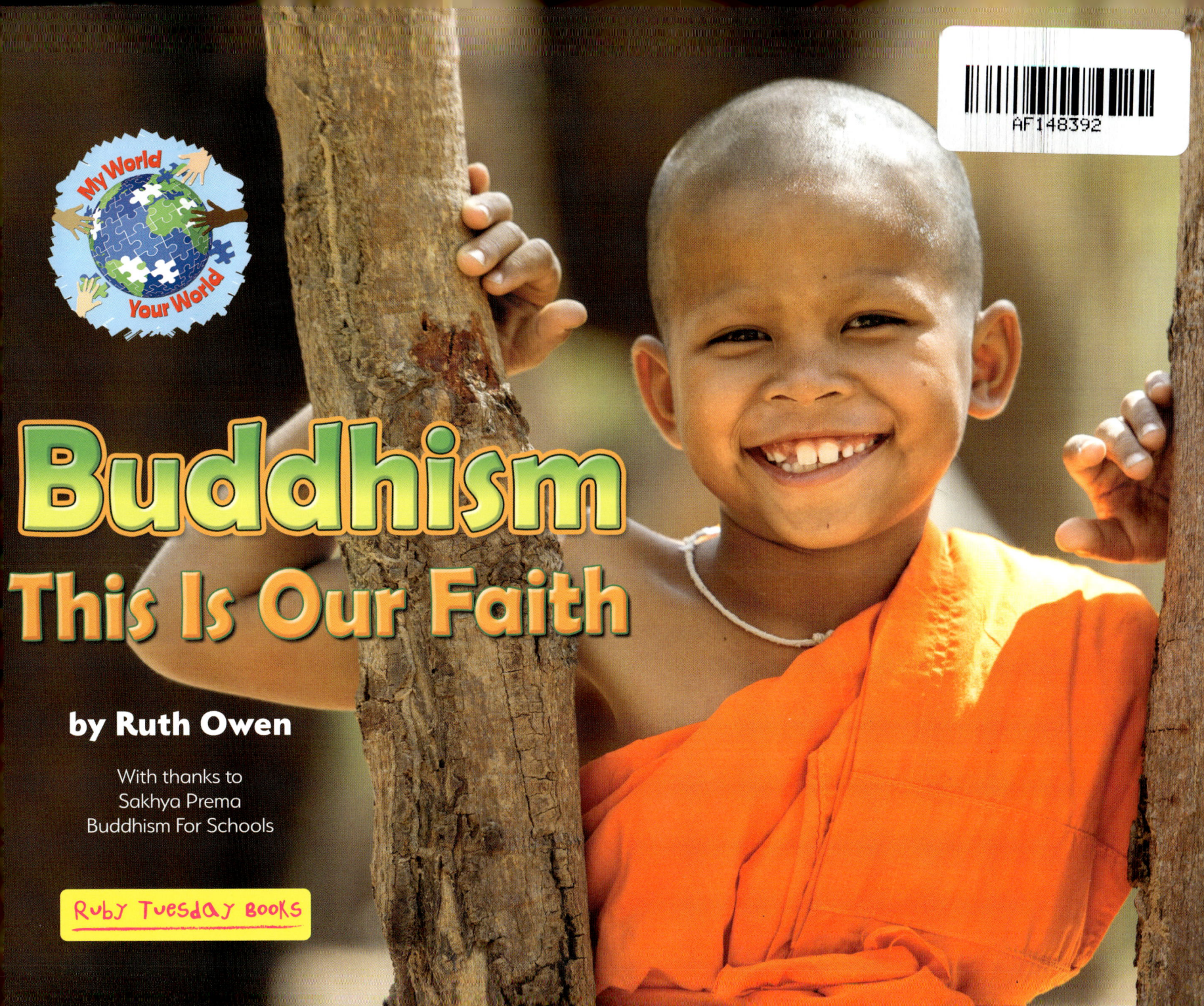

My World Your World

Buddhism
This Is Our Faith

by Ruth Owen

With thanks to
Sakhya Prema
Buddhism For Schools

Ruby Tuesday Books

Published in 2026 by Ruby Tuesday Books Ltd.

Editor: Mark J. Sachner
Design & Production: Tammy West

Photo Credits:

Alamy: Cover (Peter Schickert), 8 (Weiming Xie), 10 (imagebroker.com), 11B (Melvyn Longhurst), 15 (robertharding), 16T (Hemis), 16B (Crystite licensed), 17T (Eitan Simanor), 17B (Matthew Wakem), 19L (Hemis), 20 (Zuma Press Inc), 22 (Cynthia Lee); Godongphoto/Shutterstock/Alamy: 3, 6–7, 21; Shutterstock: 1 (Bannafarsai Stock), 2 (fokke baarssen), 4 (Ronnachai Palas), 5L (Inoprasom), 5R (nymphoenix), 9L (Artwork Kh), 9R (Tawatchaiwanasri), 11 (Stephane Bidouze/OPIS Zagreb), 12T (Chubykin Arkady), 12B (Jesse33), 13L (Hung Chung Chih), 13R (Dontree__M), 14 (Jonathan Hoseana), 18 (ball ball 123), 19R (wimammoth), 22 (Dmytro Vietrov), 23 (Huy Thoai), 24 (Baramyou0708).

British Library Cataloguing in Publication Data (CIP) is available for this title.

ISBN 978-1-78856-213-3

Printed in Malta by Gutenberg Press

www.rubytuesdaybooks.com

FSC
MIX
Paper | Supporting responsible forestry
FSC® C022612
www.fsc.org

Contents

Words shown **in bold** in the text
are explained in the glossary.

This Is Our Faith

The faith of Buddhism teaches people how to live kind and **peaceful** lives.

People who follow this faith are called Buddhists.

Buddhists do not believe in a god. They live by the teachings of a man named the Buddha, who lived about 2600 years ago.

The faith of Buddhism began in India. Most Buddhists live in Asia in countries such as Thailand, Myanmar, China, Japan and India. But there are Buddhists all over the world, including in the UK.

A Buddhist family

4

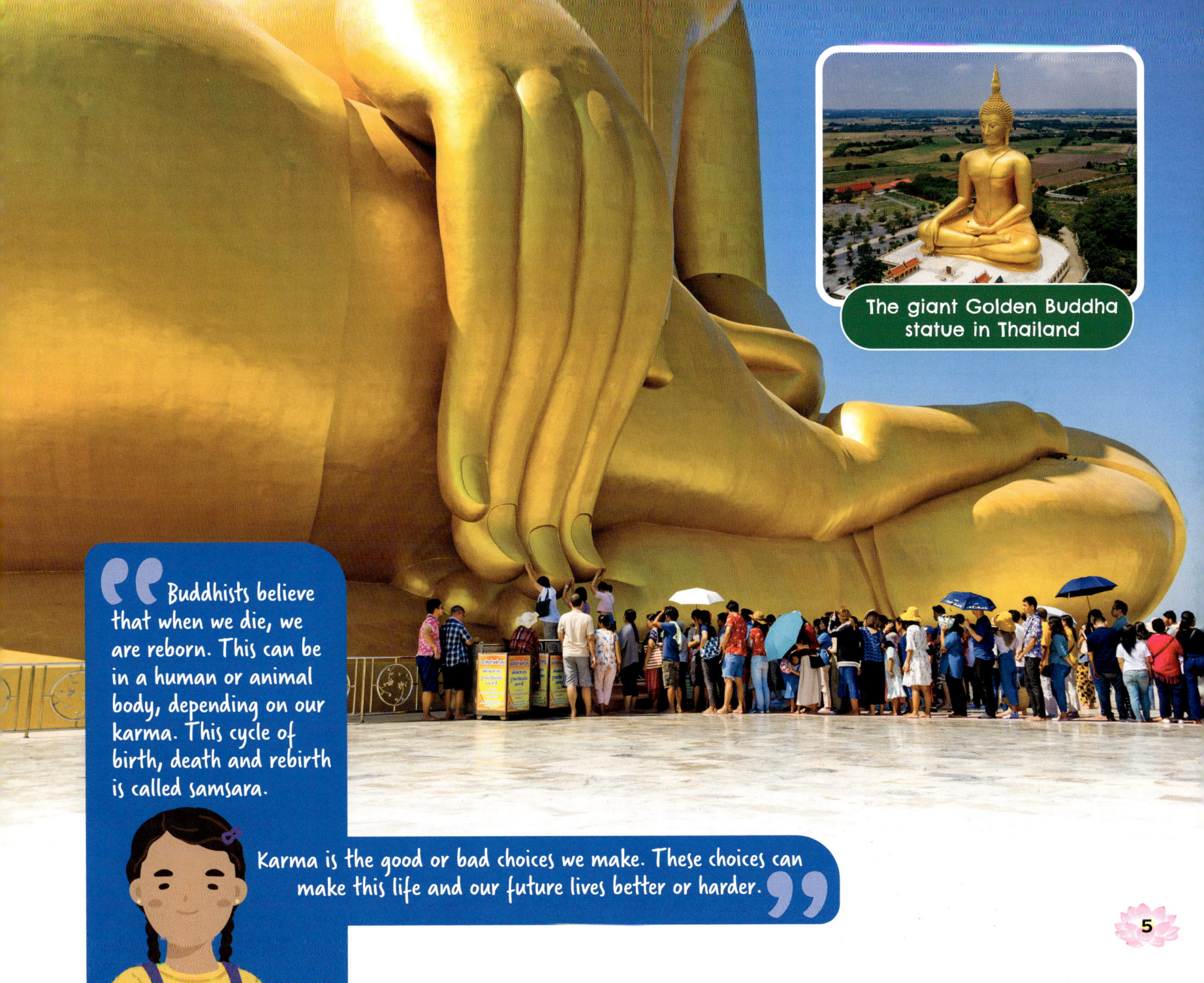

The giant Golden Buddha statue in Thailand

"Buddhists believe that when we die, we are reborn. This can be in a human or animal body, depending on our karma. This cycle of birth, death and rebirth is called samsara.

Karma is the good or bad choices we make. These choices can make this life and our future lives better or harder."

The Story of the Buddha

The Buddha was born a wealthy prince named Siddhartha Gautama.

He lived a life of luxury and did not know about suffering.

Baby prince

Siddhartha's mother, Queen Maya

Siddhartha

People suffering and dying

One day, Siddhartha left his palace and saw people who were old, ill and dying. He realised that eventually he would suffer too!

Siddhartha also saw a holy man who was calm and peaceful.

For six years, Siddhartha lived simply like the holy man. He had little food and no belongings. But he could still not find peace.

Then one day, he sat under a tree and **meditated**.

Holy man

Siddhartha meditating

The Buddha

Followers called sangha

The Buddha means "the one who is awakened".

This calm and focused way of thinking helped him find peace and become **enlightened**.

The Buddha understood how to live in a way that could lead to a **state** called **Nirvana**. Buddhists believe that when someone reaches Nirvana, the cycle of suffering and being born again will end.

Siddhartha became the Buddha and began to share his teachings.

The Buddha's Teachings

Buddhists believe that by following the Buddha's teachings they can live a kind and careful life and reach Nirvana.

"The Buddha discovered the Four Noble Truths."

There will be suffering in our lives. We get ill, people we love die and we can't always have the things we want.

We suffer because we want things. We want life to stay the same. We want to be pain free. We might want things we can't have, such as riches and fame.

Suffering can end if we stop wanting things. We should let go of greedy, jealous and angry feelings. We must accept that things change and loss is part of life.

We can stop suffering by following the Eightfold Path. When we do good things, good things happen to us, and life becomes much happier.

The Buddha's teachings are called Dharma, which means "truth and duty".

The **Eightfold Path** is a way that people can think, speak and act wisely and kindly every day.

The Eightfold Path is often shown as the Wheel of Dharma.

Wheel of Dharma

Right View
See things the way they are. Know that our actions matter.

Right Meditation
Meditate to make your mind calm, strong, focused and positive.

Right Thought
Be kind. Don't hurt others. Don't be selfish.

Right Mindfulness
Think carefully before you speak or do something.

Right Speech
Speak kindly, truthfully and positively. Do not lie, gossip or get angry.

Right Effort
Try to think and do good things. Avoid thinking or doing unkind or bad things.

Right Action
Do things that help. Don't do harm.

Right Livelihood
As an adult, do a job that does not hurt people or animals.

Wheel of Dharma

9

The Tipitaka

For a long time the Buddha's teachings were passed from person to person by word of mouth.

Then they were written down on palm tree leaves that were stored in baskets.

The **sacred** writings are called the Tipitaka, which means "three baskets".

The Tipitaka also includes stories about the Buddha's past lives. They teach how his good karma, or actions, helped him reach enlightenment.

Writings from the Tipitaka

At a **temple** in Myanmar, the Tipitaka has been **inscribed** on 729 marble slabs.

Each piece of marble stands in a small white building, called a cave.

Temple

Cave

Marble slab

Today, Buddhists can read the Buddha's words in books.

Tipitaka

Living a Buddhist Life

A very important part of a Buddhist's life is to do no harm. This is called ahimsa.

Buddhists are usually vegetarian or vegan.

A vegan stir-fry with noodles

Giving to charity is called dana.

Doing kind things for other people is also important. This is called seva.

Buddhists give money to charities to help people who are in need.

To show devotion to the Buddha, Buddhists take part in **puja**.

They meditate, **chant** and think deeply about the Buddha's teachings.

They may do this in front of a small **shrine** in their home.

A Buddhist can meditate anywhere that's quiet.

Buddhists place flowers on a shrine. As the flowers die, they are a reminder that life is beautiful, but nothing lasts forever.

A shrine with a statue of the Buddha.

"When I meditate, I take slow, deep breaths in and out. I try to make my mind calm and peaceful. Buddhists believe that meditation can help people find peace and move closer to Nirvana."

13

Welcome to a Buddhist Temple

A Buddhist temple in London

Buddhists come together to take part in puja at a temple or Buddhist centre.

People from the local community who are not Buddhists are also welcome.

Visitors may come to a temple to learn about meditation, spend time in its peaceful garden, share food and enjoy Buddhist festivals.

"Before entering the temple, we remove our shoes to keep the temple clean. We put our hands together and bow to the statue of the Buddha to show respect."

Inside a temple, there is a shrine hall with a statue of the Buddha.

People place candles, flowers, food and water on the shrine as offerings.

They meditate, chant and listen to teachings.

A shrine in a temple in Thailand

15

Buddhist Monks and Nuns

Some Buddhists choose to live a simple life of devotion to their faith.

The men who do this are monks, and the women are nuns.

Monks and nuns usually live at a temple in buildings called a **monastery**.

They spend their days meditating, chanting and studying the Buddha's teachings.

Buddhist monk

Monks and nuns also take care of the temple and do chores such as cooking and washing their robes.

Each morning, monks and nuns visit their local community to receive gifts of food, called alms.

In return, they lead puja in the temple and help their neighbours understand the Buddha's teachings.

Nuns collecting alms

Alms bowl

Monks and nuns have only a few possessions, including a bowl, their robes and a needle and thread. They have a razor for shaving their head and washing items, such as soap.

Young Monks and Nuns

Some Buddhist children spend time at a monastery living as a **novice**, or trainee, monk or nun.

They do this to learn about their faith.

Just like adult monks and nuns, the novices follow a strict routine each day.

Monks and nuns shave their heads to stay clean. It is also a reminder that how a person looks is not important.

A novice having their head shaved

The novices meditate, chant and study Buddhist teachings. They may also have lessons, such as maths and reading.

Novice monks collecting food

The novice monks have chores to do.

Children may stay at a monastery for a few days, weeks or months. Once they are 20 years old, they can choose to become a monk or nun.

"We wake at 4 am for meditation, chanting and study. Then we walk around our neighbourhood and people offer us food."

"We eat two meals each day — breakfast and lunch. For breakfast today, we had tea, rice and pickled vegetables."

Let's Celebrate! Kathina

In autumn, some Buddhists celebrate the festival of Kathina.

At this time, people bring new robes for the monks and nuns at their local temple.

They may also give food, flowers, candles, **incense** and money.

People thank the monks and nuns for guiding them, helping the community and caring for the temple.

Gifts of money are arranged on money trees.

People often form a joyful procession to carry the new robes to the temple.

A Kathina festival in Switzerland

Monk

New robes

"At Kathina, people may also give useful items such as razors, soap, medicines — and even building materials to fix the temple!"

Then people join the monks and nuns to meditate, chant and share a big vegetarian or vegan meal.

Let's Celebrate! Vesak

Vesak, or Buddha Day, is the most important Buddhist festival. It takes place in May.

Vesak celebrates the birth, enlightenment and death of the Buddha.

People visit their temple and take gifts of food, flowers, candles and incense.

These girls have made Vesak lanterns.

Food offerings at Vesak

Temples, homes and other buildings are decorated with Vesak lanterns made of paper or wood.

Some Buddhists take part in "Bathing the Buddha". They pour scented water over a statue of the baby Buddha.

This ceremony reminds people to wash away thoughts of greed and hate.

During Vesak, Buddhists make donations of food, clothes and money to people in need.

"Bathing the Buddha" at a temple in Vietnam

> Some Buddhists also celebrate Nirvana Day. We remember the day the Buddha died and achieved Nirvana. We think about one day achieving Nirvana and about loved ones who have died.

GLOSSARY

chant
In Buddhism, to say special words and names from the Buddha's teachings out loud, over and over again.

Eightfold Path (the)
The Buddha's eight guidelines for living that help people overcome suffering and move towards Nirvana.

enlightened
Becoming wise and free from greed, hatred and ignorance, like the Buddha.

Four Noble Truths (the)
The four ideas in the Buddha's teachings that explain why people suffer and how suffering can be ended.

incense
A special stick that burns slowly and makes a sweet or spicy smoke.

inscribed
Carved or written on a surface such as metal or stone.

meditate
To train your mind to be calm and quiet by sitting quietly, breathing deeply and thinking good thoughts.

monastery
The buildings where monks and nuns live and practise their faith. Men and women usually live separately.

Nirvana
In Buddhist beliefs, a state of complete peace, where a person is free from ignorance, hatred, greed and suffering. It is a peace that does not change or fade away. When someone reaches Nirvana, the cycle of suffering and rebirth comes to an end.

novice
A person who is a beginner.

peaceful
Quiet and calm, without fighting or doing harm.

puja
In Buddhism, to meditate, chant, make offerings and think about the Buddha's teachings.

sacred
Something very special and important that is respected – for example, the Buddha's teachings or a temple.

shrine
In Buddhism, a table or raised area in a home or temple where there is a statue of the Buddha and offerings. People may sit before a shrine during puja.

state
How someone feels or what someone's mind and body are like at a certain time. For example, if you feel happy, you are in a state of happiness.

temple
In Buddhism, a building where people come to practise puja, meditate and celebrate festivals.

24

INDEX

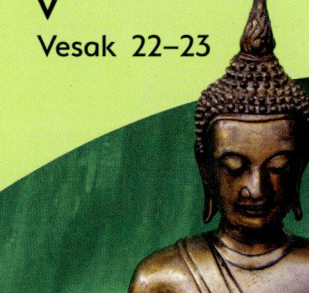